CONTENTS

Some words are shown in **bold**, like this. You can find out what they mean by looking in the glossary.

PEOPLE MAKE HISTORY

The photograph below shows an amazing individual who has made history.
This remarkable man's name is Usain Bolt, the fastest man ever to have lived.
Like every person, he has a history. And, like every famous person, there are
many ways we can find out about his personal history.

Here is Bolt, in his famous "lightning bolt" pose, after he won the final of the 200-metres at
the 2012 Olympics. This historic win is now known as "the double-triple". The "triple" part of
this is because Bolt also won the 4 x 100 metre relay final and the 100-metre final in the same
Olympics. As he had achieved this triple win at the 2008 Olympics as well, this win made it "the
double-triple".

EVERY
PERSON
HAS A HISTORY

Rebecca Vickers

raintree
a Capstone company — publishers for children

Raintree is an imprint of Capstone Global Library Limited, a company incorporated in England and Wales having its registered office at 7 Pilgrim Street, London, EC4V 6LB Registered company number: 6695582

www.raintreepublishers.co.uk
myorders@raintreepublishers.co.uk

Text © Capstone Global Library Limited 2014
First published in hardback in 2014
Paperback edition first published in 2015
The moral rights of the proprietor have been asserted.

Edited by Andrew Farrow, James Benefield, and Adrian Vigliano
Designed by Tim Bond
Original illustrations © Capstone Global Library Ltd 2014
Picture research by Liz Alexander
Originated by Capstone Global Library Ltd
Production by Victoria Fitzgerald

Printed and bound in China

ISBN 978 1 406 27275 8 (hardback)
17 16 15 14 13
10 9 8 7 6 5 4 3 2 1

ISBN 978 1 406 27280 2 (paperback)
18 17 16 15 14
10 9 8 7 6 5 4 3 2 1

British Library Cataloguing in Publication Data
A full catalogue record for this book is available from the British Library.

Acknowledgements

We would like to thank the following for permission to reproduce photographs: Alamy pp. 26 (© The Photolibrary Wales), 30 (© Andrea Heselton), 32 (© PCJones), 41 (© epa european pressphoto agency b.v.), 47 (© Archive Pics), 51 (© INTERFOTO), By Permission of the Shakespeare Birthplace Trust p. 15; Corbis pp/ 19 (John Harper), 34 (Olivier Douliery/ABACAUSA.com); Getty Images pp. 7 (Michael Steele), 9 (Prisma/UIG), pp. 16, 36 (Hulton Archive), 17 (Bloomberg News), 23 (NOEL CELIS/AFP), 25 (Mike Powell /Allsport), 27 (Mark Kauffman/Time Life Pictures), 33l (Fotosearch), 43 (New York Daily News Archive), 45 (Mark Milan/FilmMagic), 55 (JUSTIN TALLIS/AFP), Olivia Miwil p. 14; Rebecca Vickers pp. 8, 10; Reuters p. 42 (© Felix Evens); Rex Features 4, (The World of Sports SC), 21 (Moviestore Collection); Shutterstock 13 (Universal Images Group), 28, 29 (© LysFoto), 33r (© Africa Studio), 39 (Eye Ubiquitous), 49 (Blend Images), 57 (Design Pics); The National Archives, 11 (ref. RG11/ Piece: 2183/ Folio: 117/ Page: 5/ GSU roll: 1341525); The National Archives and Records Administration, 11b.

Cover photograph: Family looking at family tree reproduced with the permission of Corbis (© Matt Bird); Wilma Rudolph with Dorothy Hyman reproduced with the permission of Getty Images (Rolls Press/Popperfoto); Little girl blowing out candles reproduced with the permission of Superstock (ClassicStock.com); Mother with her daughter looking at their photo album reproduced with the permission of Shutterstock (© wavebreakmedia).

Every effort has been made to contact copyright holders of material reproduced in this book. Any omissions will be rectified in subsequent printings if notice is given to the publisher.

The "Lightning Bolt" backstory

Usain Bolt was born in Jamaica in 1986 at Sherwood Content in the rural area of Trelawny parish. His parents had a small local food shop. Bolt played football and cricket with his brother along the road outside their house. He had no dreams or ambitions for his life, or expectations for the future. The only thing he thought about was playing sport every day. With his relaxed attitude to life and love of practical jokes, Bolt did not seem to have the dedication and determination needed to become a first-class athlete. Luckily, his natural talent, together with the hard work and understanding of his coaches, took Usain Bolt to success on the world athletics stage.

When people are famous enough for us to have heard of them, they will probably have lived at least a fifth of their lives. Their history will have already started. Their family background, personal ambitions, and the places they live will all have contributed to the growing story of their lives.

Usain Bolt's history could have been limited by lack of focus and a jokey, unserious nature. But this didn't happen. Instead, it was the start of a journey that would make him an international sporting sensation. By late August in 2012, when his involvement in the London Olympic Games had finished, this smiling sprinter had gained more gold medals. Bolt truly made history, even though most of his life is still to come!

Zoom in: The Lightning Bolt's coaches

Athletes need to find someone to help them reach their full potential. When one of Usain Bolt's schoolteachers realized how fast Usain could run, he put the young teenager in touch with coach Pablo McNeill. McNeill guided Bolt from a young age until he became a professional athlete in 2004. During this next year, through his first Olympic performance in Athens in 2004, Bolt was coached by somebody else, Fitz Coleman. Then, after only a year, Coleman was replaced by Glen Mills, who is still Bolt's coach today. Mills has worked hard to make Bolt take his career seriously and helped him develop physically and mentally. Bolt says that Mills can always find ways he can improve Bolt's performance in a race and get even faster.

History research needs evidence

Everything that happened to Usain Bolt during his childhood, teenage years, and early athletics career changed the speedy, sport-mad little boy into a man who caught the attention of the world. From his parents' names to his first successes, to his incredible world records, Bolt's history can be researched and unravelled.

To find out about someone's life, such as Usain Bolt's, you need **reliable evidence**. Evidence is anything you can discover and examine that tells you about the subject being researched. It comes in different forms, from books to photographs. A **primary source** is a piece of evidence from the time in history when something happened, for example a photograph taken of Bolt at school. When evidence is created later, for example a recent magazine article about Bolt's early life, then it is a **secondary source**.

All evidence needs to be **evaluated** for its importance and reliability. Are the photographs on page seven (including the one featured in the screenshot at the bottom of the page) really of Bolt? How can you be sure? If they are on his official website, or in his **autobiography**, then they probably are of him. What are the sources where we might have to question reliability?

Zoom in: Can one person's life tell you about others?

Finding out about the history of one person can be a great jumping off point for finding out about others who share a similar history. As well as famous people, ordinary men and women can give us insights into the past. They might have performed certain important jobs, experienced great world events, or lived in particular places. Bolt's early life is interesting because of what he has become, as an international athletics superstar. Researching Bolt can also provide general information about life in rural Jamaica in the 1990s and the training of sportsmen and sportswomen.

Primary source evidence

Photographs like this one of a teenage Bolt, snapped in 2002, are direct evidence from the time they were taken. As well as the image, a photograph can show **context** and background, such as specific locations or family members. It provides clues about lifestyles and how people want themselves to be portrayed. But photographs as evidence also raise questions:

- Who took the photograph and why?
- Was the shot posed or taken spontaneously?
- Why were you able to find this photograph? Are other photographs of the person not available to researchers?

Secondary source evidence

"With no street lights and limited running water, walking through Sherwood Content is like going back in time where old men ride donkeys ... and everyone waves at passing cars."

(*Usain Bolt's Rise From Rags to Riches*, Anna Kessel, *The Observer*, 9 August 2009)

This secondary source quote is from a British newspaper story about Bolt's early life.

Where should I look?

When you are researching someone who is doing more things every day, you need to use sources that are regularly updated. Famous people usually have their own approved websites, Twitter feeds, and blogs.

Remember, official sites only tell you what the person wants the public to know. If someone does something embarrassing, or even illegal, this information will probably not be on the site!

WHO IS THAT?
THE MYSTERIOUS RELATIVE

The metal identification label on the exotic plant in the Singapore Botanic Gardens gave the scientific name of a member of the ginger family: *Pleuranthodium foxworthyi*. This was the first clue used by American tourist Barb Carson in a search for a mysterious, previously unknown, **ancestor**. The search ended up covering four continents; family history websites; birth, marriage, and death records; and also national **census** returns.

This metal plant ID tag with the plant name *Pleuranthodium foxworthyi* is the evidence that started the search for Fred Foxworthy. This is the picture that Barb took of the plant label, using her mobile phone's camera.

Finding family

The second part of a Latin name like *Pleuranthodium foxworthyi* often refers to the person who identifies and names the plant for scientific purposes. This was what first caught the attention of American tourist Barb in Singapore. She knew that her grandmother's surname was also Foxworthy. So who was the person that gave the family name to a plant in South East Asia? Was this mystery person a relative?

Historical research is not just useful for finding out about the famous and important. Most people, no matter how ordinary, leave some **documents** behind as evidence of their lives. All important life events, such as birth and death, are officially recorded. Schools, universities, hospitals, and employers keep records. Governments also keep track of their citizens at national and local level. There are official records for many stages of life, from census returns to tax records.

Barb hoped she would find something like this. She would be able to use this sea of information to track down the person with the surname of Foxworthy who named the ginger plant.

Introducing Dr Fred Foxworthy

When you need to find out about a person, the internet is now a good place to start. When Barb typed the Latin name of the ginger plant into a search engine, she found out it had been called "foxworthyi" after a botanist (someone who studies plants) and tropical forestry expert called Dr Fred W. Foxworthy. The information pointed to him being a British **colonial civil servant** who had been based in the Straits Settlements (now Singapore and Malaysia). Could he have any connection to Barb's grandmother, in the United States? She was about to find this out.

Zoom in: Botanists and plant collectors

During the 18th and 19th centuries, many plant collectors from Europe and North America travelled the world to identify and bring home exciting and exotic plants. Some of these, such as food crop plants, could be grown for economic purposes. Others were collected for their beauty. Tropical orchids were particularly sought after and fetched a high price when taken back to the collectors' home countries.

Many 18th and 19th century people from Europe and North America, such as naturalists and geographers, travelled the world to discover new things. This is Alexander von Humboldt, a German naturalist and geographer. He explored many places in South America.

Following the census trail

So, where to look now? Barb didn't know the names of Fred's parents, or when or where he was born. The indexed national census returns are a good primary source to search when this is the case. See the box below to learn more about these. Barb knew that Fred Foxworthy was working in South East Asia in the early 1900s, so she searched the 1871, 1881, and 1891 British census indexes for his name. Unfortunately, she had no luck.

To be thorough, Barb decided to try the US national census indexes for the same period. And there he was! Fred was listed with his family in the 1880 census for the state of Illinois. Armed with Fred's father's name, Barb was able to look at her grandmother's **family tree** and confirm that Fred was her great-grandfather's cousin.

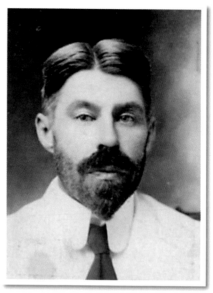

This is an old, rare photo of Dr Fred W. Foxworthy (1877–1950). Barb found out about him by searching census information and looking through her grandmother's family tree. It shows that there can be all kinds of surprises in your family's history.

What is a census?   *i*

A national census is the official counting and recording of information about people that national governments regularly carry out. In many developed countries, these have been organized at 10-year intervals for the last 200 years. The information taken down has changed through time, but these documents can be very useful. Historic census returns for many countries have been indexed by name and are available to view on the internet. The information that appears on census returns contains details that may be private or sensitive. Because of this, British census returns are only made public after 100 years and the US census returns after 70 years.

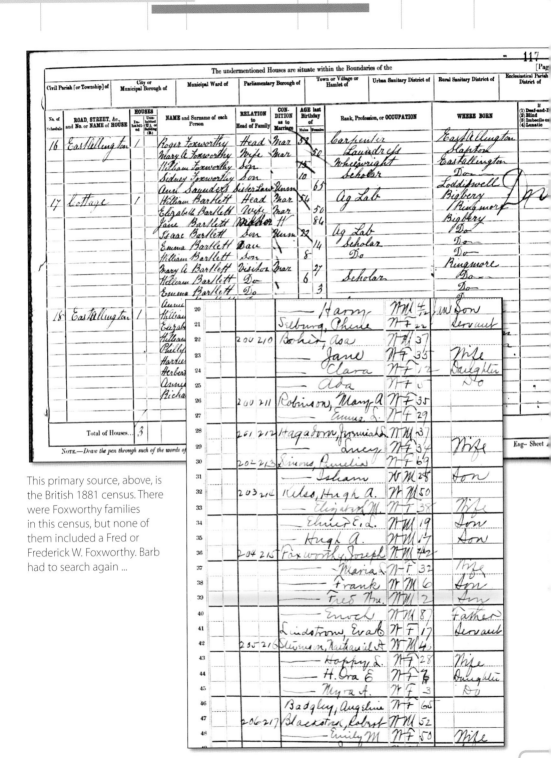

This primary source, above, is the British 1881 census. There were Foxworthy families in this census, but none of them included a Fred or Frederick W. Foxworthy. Barb had to search again ...

This primary source, above, is the US 1880 census. In the highlighted line, you can see Fred's name. Three lines up is his family's name.

Finding out about Fred

Making the family connection was just the beginning of the story. Now Barb needed to put flesh on the bones of this mysterious ancestor. How did a boy born in Illinois end up as a British civil servant in Southeast Asia? Had he ever returned to the United States? Did he have **descendants**?

Genealogy on TV *i*

Over the last few years, family history research has become very popular. For example, there are now television series where **genealogists** help celebrities find out about their ancestors. You can get helpful hints from the techniques they use. Check these websites for more information about genealogists and these shows:

www.bbc.co.uk/whodoyouthinkyouare

www.findmypast.co.uk

www.pbs.org/wnet/finding-your-roots

Hatched, matched, and dispatched

Armed with the census information, Barb was able to use birth, marriage, and death records to find out more about Fred's early life. These primary sources, known in slang terms as hatch (birth), match (marriage), and dispatch (death) records, became a legal requirement in many countries during the 1800s. In the UK, **civil registration** of these life events started in 1837. Before this, records were mainly kept by churches and synagogues.

Fred's **obituary** gave Barb further information about his education at Cornell University in New York State, so she was able to follow up these records. His travels overseas, first to the Philippines and then to the British colony, the Straits Settlement, were documented in the books he wrote (about the plant life of the regions he explored). In Singapore, Fred was employed by the British government as Senior Forestry Officer. This all explained how he appeared as British on some records, despite always being an American citizen.

Barb also found books and articles that were helpful. Some were written by Fred Foxworthy about plant life in national and university library catalogues. She also found him mentioned in secondary sources, such as histories of the Straits Settlement and books about botanists and plant collectors.

Today, rubber trees are prepared for tapping using Henry Ridley's method. This means that the trees can survive after being tapped for their liquid latex, or rubber.

Research roadshow:
Sir Henry "Rubber" Ridley

One of the most important of the botanists who went to South East Asia was Henry N. Ridley (1855–1956). Although the rubber tree was native to Brazil, it was being planted in other tropical areas. Everyone wanted rubber for its uses in manufacturing and it would become increasingly important for the growing automobile industry. It was hard to grow rubber trees successfully. Getting the liquid latex (rubber) out of the tree usually killed it. In 1895, Ridley developed a method for tapping a tree and extracting the latex without destroying the tree. Giving out seeds and plants he grew himself, Ridley was able to convince farmers on the Malay Peninsula to farm this valuable crop. He became known as "Rubber" Ridley, and was later knighted by the British government.

What Fred did next

Barb found out that Fred did not marry until he was in his late fifties. Also, Fred did not have any children. He returned to the United States in the 1930s after working in South East Asia for 30 years. His wife Laura was from Iowa, Barb's home state. When Fred died, he was buried in the cemetery near Laura's former home. Laura died a few years afterward and was buried next to Fred.

Searching the internet

Barb found the last exciting pieces of the puzzle in an internet search. Her search brought her attention to academic papers and **archive** material relating to Fred held in Malaysia, Singapore, and at the University of California in North America.

But that was not all. Surprisingly, there were also original journals and drawings made on his plant-hunting expeditions in a museum in Australia. Indeed, when he died he even had an obituary published in the academic science journal *Nature*.

Fred Foxworthy has now been added to Barb Carson's family tree as a distinguished ancestor. He is no longer a "mysterious relative".

In 1921, Fred helped choose the land where the Forestry Research Institute of Malaysia (FRIM) was developed. He became its first Chief Research Officer. FRIM is still considered to be one of the best tropical forestry institutes in the world. Although Fred left South East Asia over 80 years ago, his name lives on in "Jalan Foxworthy" (Foxworthy Road) at FRIM – see the picture above!

Where should I look?

Maybe you have a Fred Foxworthy in your family, someone no one really knows about. You could try some of the same sources Barb examined, such as census returns; birth, marriage, and death registrations; obituaries; newspapers; and university records to solve your own family mysteries. A lot of this information is available online, but there are also local history libraries, county record offices or archives, and specialist family history research centres. Other useful sources include:

- Family bibles and family trees that list life events and connections
- Official or church documents, such as birth, marriage, or death certificates
- Information from relatives, particularly elderly relatives
- Other people's research. If you are lucky, someone else might have researched the same person and published or put the research online.

Remember, the same types of documentary evidence used to research the lives of well-known people can be used to trace your own ancestors. Famous people may appear in more varied pieces of evidence, but they were all born and they all died, and many will have married.

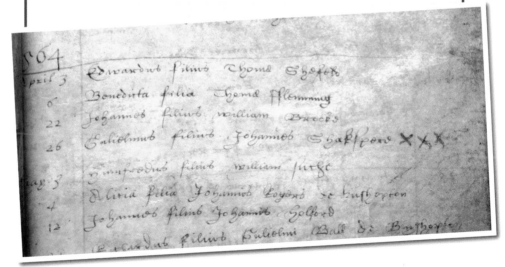

Important and famous people like playwright William Shakespeare leave the same trail of evidence as ordinary people. This entry in the church records of Stratford-upon-Avon from 1564 records the baptism of William Shakespeare, son of John Shakespeare. It is recorded in the fourth line down under "1564", on 26 April.

OFFICIAL RECORDS: EDUCATION AND THE MILITARY

By the time World War II ended in 1945, British Prime Minister Winston Churchill (1874–1965) was one of the best-known people in the world. He had successfully led his country through five years of turmoil. He had spent the previous 44 years in the public eye, most of them as a politician and member of the British Parliament. However, although Churchill was not famous for the first 27 years of his life, he left behind evidence in official records during this time.

Could do better

For as long as schools, colleges, and universities have existed, they have kept records relating to their students and staff. For Winston Churchill, his school days were probably the least successful part of his life. But records of his time at school still exist. Churchill's father certainly received a number of bad school reports and letters from teachers about his son. Since the technology existed, schools and universities have also taken photographs of their students and of school activities, such as sports and social events. All of these records are useful primary sources for historical research.

Historical school records are also very good sources of **social history** information. In most countries, government authorities have always required

publicly funded schools to keep thorough records. Details about attendance, illness, behaviour, and parental involvement can all be used to help recreate what life was really like at a specific time. Many of the **logbooks** kept by head teachers in English schools go into great detail about local and national events, including the weather.

Young Winston Churchill (shown here in his school uniform) hated having to learn Latin and Greek at school, and always did badly in these subjects. He loved English and history and was particularly good at memorization.

Winston Churchill often had to write to his parents to explain his bad school reports. His school thought he wasn't working to his ability, but Churchill himself understood what his problem was: "Where my reason, imagination, or interest was not engaged, I would not or could not learn."

Zoom in: When did people have to go to school?

All of Winston Churchill's education took place in selective, quite expensive, private schools. During the 19th century, many countries decided that governments should provide money to build schools and hire teachers. Once funding was given to education, laws were passed saying that children had to attend. Scotland had introduced **compulsory** school attendance by 1696, but England and Wales were among the last European countries to have an Education Act. It was passed in 1870, and, in 1880, the leaving age was raised to 10! It was later raised in stages to 13, then to 15, and then 16. In September 2013, the leaving age for full-time education rose to 17.

A military evidence trail

When Winston Churchill was accepted into army officer training at the Royal Military College at Sandhurst, his life started to be documented in yet another set of official records. After finishing at Sandhurst, Churchill was appointed as a lieutenant in the army cavalry unit called the Queen's Own Hussars, and his military service record started. Every time he changed a posting or took part in a military engagement, this information was added to his military records. Any wounds received, or medals won, were also added.

In many countries, all members of the military have a personal service record. But wider information about units and regiments can also be found in military logbooks and war diaries, and the **dispatches** sent back from war zones.

Military records

You can also research information about soldiers and sailors from the period before World War I. There are very full military records for the American Civil War (1861–1865), the Boer War (1899–1902), and the Crimean War (1853–1856). By the mid-19th century, countries such as the United Kingdom and the United States had professional armies and navies as well as local **militia**.

Before this, in the United Kingdom there were only a few regular army regiments. Other soldiers were gathered from the local militia when conflicts started and fighting men were required. The names of these local fighters were listed for many years on documents known as muster rolls. A number of these have been typed out and indexed, and some are available online.

Where should I look?

In the UK, the Imperial War Museum (**www.iwm.org.uk**) and the National Army Museum (**www.nam.ac.uk**) can be visited in person or online. Most of the historic British army regiments have regimental associations with museums. You can find out more about the regiments Winston Churchill was associated with by going to the website of the Queen's Own Hussars (**www.thequeensownhussars.co.uk**) and the Queen's Royal Lancers (**www.qrlassociation.co.uk**). For information about the museums and websites for other regiments, try searching (**www.armymuseums.org.uk**).

Military museums, like the Imperial War Museum (IWM), shown here, hold huge collections of written documents and objects relating to individuals and their military service. Personal papers, letters, journals, and diaries of members of all the different branches of the military have been donated to the IWM. This hall at the museum shows some of the American and British equipment used during World War II.

Zoom in: Protected information

All of Winston Churchill's military records are available for researchers and as part of the online search services of the UK National Archives. This is because Churchill was not on active service during World War II. Officially, current regulations do not allow anyone but the person themselves or, if they are dead, their nearest relative, to receive copies of service records from World War II to the present.

From five sailors to one soldier

In 1998, a film based around the **Allies'** D-Day invasion of Normandy in World War II was released to critical acclaim. It ended up winning five Academy Awards, including one for its director, Steven Spielberg. The film, *Saving Private Ryan*, is sometimes named by critics as one of the best war films ever made.

Although this film is a work of fiction, its inspiration comes from a real family tragedy. In November 1942, the US navy cruiser USS *Juneau* sank in the Pacific Ocean near the Solomon Islands, during the Battle of Guadalcanal. Six hundred and eighty-seven men lost their lives. Among those who perished were the five Sullivan brothers from Waterloo, Iowa.

To avoid a repetition of such a tragedy, extra care was taken to make sure brothers would no longer be allowed to serve together. This was used by Robert Rodat, writer of *Saving Private Ryan*, as the focus of the film's plot: two brothers from one family have been killed in action, and the remaining brother has to be "saved" and returned home. When the officer charged with finding Private Ryan has the situation explained to him, the example given of what needs to be avoided is the loss of the five Sullivan brothers.

The Sullivan brothers, shown above, were named George, Frank, Joseph, Matt, and Al.

The story of the deaths of the Sullivan brothers was one of the inspirations for the Hollywood film *Saving Private Ryan*.

Zoom in: From real life to the big screen

Individuals often write accounts of their lives in the form of autobiographies. Also, people who have led interesting lives or become famous may have books written about them by others. Some of these sources are adapted for television or made into films. They can provide interesting insights into the people portrayed, although they may not be factually or historically accurate. **Biopics** that have been applauded by film critics and historians include:

- *Lincoln* (2012) which is about Abraham Lincoln, and is adapted from the book *Team of Rivals* by Doris Kearns Goodwin.

- *Miss Potter* (2006) which is about Beatrix Potter, and is adapted from the book of the same name by Richard Maltby, Jr.

- *JFK* (1991) which is about the assassination of John F. Kennedy, and is adapted from the book *On the Trail of the Assassins* by Jim Garrison.

- *The Last Emperor* (1987) which is about the last Chinese monarch Pu Yi, and is adapted from the autobiography *From Emperor to Citizen* by Aisin-Gioro Pu Yi.

Remembering those who serve in the military

Immediately after their death in action, the Sullivan brothers became famous because of their family's great loss. Within a year, a navy vessel had been named after them, a Hollywood film had been made about their lives, and in their home town, a hospital ward and a local park were named after them. Ten years after their deaths, a row of five apple trees on the lawn of the White House in Washington DC was dedicated to the memory of the Sullivan brothers.

In towns and cities all over the world, there are war **memorials** that list the names of local people who died while serving their countries. In some places, the names for all conflicts are on one memorial, while other places have different memorials for different wars. There are also memorials with a national focus, like the **Cenotaph** in London, UK, the Tomb of the Unknown Soldier in Arlington National Cemetery, Virginia, USA, and the Australia War Memorial in that country's capital city, Canberra.

One of the most striking war memorials in the world is the Vietnam Veterans Memorial (VVM) in Washington DC, USA. It is a national monument that recognizes the great personal sacrifice of those involved. It lists the names of all those who lost their lives or were recorded as missing in action in the Vietnam War (fought between, roughly, 1955 and 1975 in and around the South East Asian country of the same name). The memorial lists over 58,000 names and is also known as "The Wall". Find out more about VVM and how its design was chosen on the internet by using a search engine.

Identifying mystery soldiers

We know which regiments Winston Churchill served in, as this information has been recorded, and we know that the Sullivan brothers were in the US Navy and which ship they served on. But what if you are trying to find out about the military service of someone based only on a photograph, uniform, or medals? How can you find out where and when they served?

There are books and websites where uniforms from different branches of the military throughout time are illustrated. Identification can be difficult, however, because old photographs are black and white, and the quality of the images is often poor. Sometimes a very small difference in a lapel or sleeve can help identify a specific regiment.

Soldiers, sailors, and airmen who have lost their lives in action far from home are usually buried in military cemeteries near where they died. This cemetery is in the Philippines and is for military personnel from the United Kingdom, United States, Canada, Australia, and India. If you want to research the grave of a member of the military who died abroad, you can search the following websites using the name of the person you are looking for: The Commonwealth War Graves Commission (**www.cwgc.org**) and the American Battle Monuments Commission (**www.abmc.gov**).

Where should I look?

If you have a piece of uniform or a photograph or painting of someone in a uniform that you want to identify, there are books for different time periods and many illustrated internet sites. For British uniforms, try looking on the following website:
www.britishempire.co.uk/forces/armyuniforms/uniform.htm

If you have an American Civil War uniform that needs identifying, the online version of Dr Howard Lanham's comprehensive book on the uniforms of the Union Army can be found by going to the site **http://howardlanham.tripod.com/newindex.html**. There are numerous books and websites that illustrate military medals. National and local museums also often have displays of medals from different conflicts throughout history.

WHERE ARE THEY NOW?

An unlikely Olympian

When a young African man took part in the swimming heats at the 2000 Summer Olympic Games in Sydney, Australia, he was unprepared for the news he would create. He wasn't a good swimmer; in fact, he had never had a chance to swim 100 metres in an Olympic-sized pool until he arrived in Sydney. But Eric Moussambani from Equatorial Guinea was about to cause a media storm and make history. He might have only been famous for a short time, but you can still find out about Eric and research what happened to him next.

A household name

Eric did not wow the crowds with his skills as a swimmer, but he did impress them and the media with the fact that he was there at all. False starts and disqualifications meant he had to swim his heat alone in the pool, and even then he did not make the fast time necessary to go on to the next round. But he did make a personal best time, and charmed the crowds with this effort and his happiness at taking part – an example of the true Olympic spirit.

Eric, now called "Eric the Eel" by the press, became an immediate celebrity. He was interviewed by over 100 news crews from around the world. He even had to have his own press assistant, provided by the Games' organizers.

The "Eel" reappears

Once the Olympics were over, Eric received some help and funding, but he was "lost" from the public gaze. Newspapers next reported what was happening with him as the Olympics in Athens approached four years later. But although Eric had improved his times enormously, his national government did not enter him properly and he could not compete.

Eric retired from swimming after that disappointment. Just before the 2012 London Olympics, Eric was in the news again. He had been appointed the official national swimming coach for Equatorial Guinea! He now trains 36 swimmers regularly as well as working a full-time job in IT for an oil company. Unfortunately, his team were not good enough to make it to the 2012 Olympics.

At the 2000 Olympics, Equatorial Guinea swimmer Eric "the Eel" Moussambani caught the attention of the press and public.

Recluses who want to get lost

Eric Moussambani's celebrity status helped him to progress in his sport. But some writers, actors, and musicians who gain fame wish it had never happened. They try to hide away from the public gaze and keep their lives to themselves. The 20th century actress Greta Garbo famously said, "I want to be alone" when she was at the height of her popularity. Other famous **recluses** include J.D. Salinger, who wrote *Catcher in the Rye*, billionaire Howard Hughes, and chess grandmaster Bobby Fisher.

However, some people who try to hide away, such as the singer Michael Jackson, attract even more attention, especially because rumours start to spread. It means their occasional media appearances are given even more attention by the press.

Zoom in: How do people get lost?

Sometimes people are not really lost. Like Eric, they are no longer interesting to the media and disappear from view. Family members can also lose touch and even good friends can end up without one another's contact information. People also end up separated from family and loved ones as **displaced persons**. This can happen for many reasons.

Wars and conflicts cause people to move to safety. Some families have lived in refugee camps for several generations. Natural disasters and environmental factors, such as earthquakes, volcanoes, hurricanes, and tsunamis, have led to people becoming displaced. Some have to leave their countries. In other cases, such as with the aftermath of 2002's Hurricane Katrina in the United States, people have to live to live in their own countries as refugees (another word for a displaced person). Some people leave their homes to escape **persecution** caused by their **ethnicity**, or their religious or political beliefs. Forced migration makes some groups go to other regions. They are physically removed from their homelands and made to live elsewhere.

People desperately searched this information wall after the 26 December 2006 tsunami to find news of missing loved ones. If you are trying to find someone, the Salvation Army helps to trace missing people. See their website **www. salvationarmy.org.uk/uki/FamilyTracing**. The International Red Cross also helps families to find each other.

Wilma Rudolph was a teenager when she participated in the 1956 Olympic Games. She is shown here winning the 100 metre sprint at the 1960 Olympics in Rome, one of her three gold medal victories during the Games.

Remembering Wilma Rudolph

Today, many national track teams contain talented athletes of all races and ethnic backgrounds. This has not always been the case. When the African American runner Wilma Rudolph took part in the 1956 Olympics, she was only 16 years old. She had overcome not only racial prejudice, but also life-threatening illness and poverty to get to the Games. At the 1960 Olympics in Rome, Italy, Wilma became the first US woman to win three gold medals.

But what happened next? A quick internet search helps find the answers. The number of black runners increased year by year, and Wilma and her achievements faded away as new stars took centre stage. Wilma became a teacher and track coach after retiring from athletics. She tragically died from a brain tumour aged only 54.

DEAD, BUT NOT FORGOTTEN

Few people live and die without making some impact on the world or without leaving at least small amounts of evidence to their existence. Others leave this world having made a huge impact on our daily lives.

From personal name to place name

In 1677, the wealthy English **Quaker** William Penn left his home country. He hoped he could get away from religious persecution to start a new life in the American colonies. Most people made the long journey to America hoping they could start a new life in a new country. Penn was much luckier. He arrived as the owner and virtual ruler of massive areas of land in what are now the US states of New Jersey, Delaware and, of course, Pennsylvania.

When Penn and large numbers of fellow Quakers arrived, he had started calling his colony Sylvania, which means "area of woods". Later, the English king, Charles II, insisted that the land be known as "Pennsylvania" because of money and friendship he had received from Penn's father, Admiral Sir William Penn. Later, Pennsylvania was one of the 13 original colonies, and it was in the first group that became states after independence.

William Penn (second from right) had a very good relationship with the Native American tribes in the lands he acquired from the British government.

These falls may look angelic, but they are not named for their heavenly beauty. They are called Angel Falls after the US pilot Jimmie Angel who first spotted them from his small plane in 1933. Angel Falls is in Venezuela, South America.

Rich man to statesman to pauper

Unfortunately, things did not work out the way William Penn had hoped for his Quaker colony in America. Even though he became the colony governor, infighting and business and money problems drove Penn back to England. His last years were spent in poverty and illness. At his death in 1718, he was buried in an unmarked pauper's grave. Do you know of any other famous figures who have shared a similar fate, either from history or perhaps in more recent times?

Traces left behind

Some famous people are remembered only by the things that are written about them. Others, like Penn, have physical monuments dedicated to them or places named after them. So, what concrete legacy did William Penn leave behind, besides the obvious family connection to the name of the state, Pennsylvania?

- Education: There are at least five schools (in the UK and the United States), one school district, and one university named after William Penn.

- Health and well-being: In Buckinghamshire, there is a swimming pool and leisure centre that bears Penn's name. In Pennsylvania, there are two hospitals named after him.

- Statues and memorials: All Hallows Church in London, where Penn was baptized, has a large memorial wall plaque in his honour. In the United States, there are at least five statues of William Penn.

- Other: There are also three cemeteries, two museums, and a memorial fire tower all named after Penn.

Former political prisoner, South African president, and campaigner against **apartheid**, Nelson Mandela has had his name memorialized all over the world.

Making a connection: Local heroes equal local names

All over the world, names given to streets, buildings, schools, and hospitals can reflect the lives of local people. Perhaps someone gave the money for a school to be built which now bears his or her name. Maybe they became famous after they left home, and their local area wants to remember a favourite son or daughter. Also, property developers often use family names when they are building new housing areas.

If there is a name used for a building or a road in your local area, and you don't know why, you can use local history museums and libraries to research the answer. Some towns and cities have had books written about their development. These secondary sources will mention the people who were important to the area's growth. People like this are often the ones who leave their legacy in the use of their names. For example, In Coventry in the West Midlands, there is a street called Henry Parkes Road. Henry Parkes (1815–1896) was a local man who gained fame as the founder of the Australian Federation, which eventually became the country of Australia. That's a long way from Coventry!

Whose name?

Some places are named in honour of rulers or important political figures, such as the US state of Maryland (for Queen Henrietta Maria, wife of King Charles I) or Charles De Gaulle Airport in Paris (after a former French president). Others are named after the people who previously owned the land or explored the area. Some places are named for the leaders of the original native inhabitants.

Place	Named after
Washington DC	US president, George Washington
Tasmania, Australia	Explorer, Abel Tasman
Angel Falls, Venezuela	Pilot, Jimmie Angel
Mexico	Aztec leader, Mexitili
Livingstone, Zambia	**Missionary**, David Livingstone

Evidence in stone

William Penn did not have a gravestone or any memorial to his passing at the time of his death, but one was later erected. The gravestones in cemeteries, as well as memorials in churches, can provide evidence for historical research. Sometimes the details for entire families can appear on a large gravestone.

You can find a lot of information in burial grounds. Information such as birth and death dates, causes of death, children's names, and even facts about an individual's profession or military service can be listed. Historically, most burial places were attached to places of worship (churchyards). In remote areas, families often had burial grounds for family members, while in bigger towns and cities the local authorities put aside land for use as cemeteries.

Many cemeteries have records of the burials they contain. In some places, groups of volunteers map all the graves, recording the information that is readable from each monument. These documents are then lodged in local libraries and churches, or made available for sale or on the internet. There are also websites with churchyard and cemetery information, such as **www.ukbmd.org.uk** and **www.findagrave.com**. These give inscriptions from graves and sometimes even photographs. There are also lists of graveyards and cemeteries in specific areas, including ones that are very old and no longer used.

Penn's grave in Buckinghamshire now has a stone, although he was so poor at the time of his death that he was buried in a pauper's grave. The third and fourth line of the stone has faded over time, but says, "Hannah Penn, 1726".

Levi Strauss was eight when he went to the United States, with his mother and his two sisters. He is an example of a true immigrant success story.

"Waist overalls"

Levi jeans are worn all over the world and are one of the most internationally recognized brand names. Few people think about the fact that the product name is in fact the name of a person, Levi Strauss (1829–1902). Strauss and a partner received a patent in 1873 for the jeans, and soon started manufacturing the blue jeans that were first called "waist overalls". His fascinating life is tied into the history of immigration to the US state of California. You can find out about Levi Strauss using various secondary sources, such as books, encyclopaedias, and biographical dictionaries.

Research roadshow: A person or a product?

People who invent, discover, or manufacture products often find their names used. However, over time, the name becomes much more identified with the product than the person. When people drive their Ford cars, they probably do not think about industrialist Henry Ford (1863–1947). When they pay their bills, banker James Barclay (1708–1766) and his place in the history of finance is not on their minds!

LEAVING AND ARRIVING

When a sickly child moved with her parents and sister halfway around the world in 1966, she became a **migrant**. Her parents made a decision that life could be better somewhere else. By doing this, they became an example of the process that started when the first human beings spread across the world from Africa.

The child, Julia Gillard, was born in Wales in 1961. When she was only five, she and her family left the UK for the warmer climate of Australia. After arriving, Julia attended school, then university, and started adult life in her adopted country. Just before Julia's 50th birthday, she became the first female Australian prime minister.

Julia Gillard, shown here with President Barack Obama, during a visit to the United States. Julia Gillard is a migrant who made the most of the chances that life in her new country gave her. As a lawyer and then as a politician, she eventually rose to the highest political office in Australia.

> ### *Zoom in: Julia Gillard's "firsts"*
> - First female leader of the Australian Labour Party.
> - First female prime minister of Australia. She became prime minister in June 2010. She was succeeded in June 2013 by Kevin Rudd.
> - First foreign-born person in 87 years to become prime minister of Australia.

Why leave home?

Over the centuries, people have chosen to become migrants for a variety of reasons:

- Religious persecution: Many different groups of people chose to move from one place to another for religious reasons. In the 17th and 18th centuries, Christian groups, such as early Protestants, Puritans, and French Huguenots, started new lives in different places (many European Jews did this too). They hoped they would be safer and able to practise their religions without any interference.

- Economic improvements: Some migrants move to escape poverty or go to where there are more job opportunities. This is still a huge motivation for migrants around the world today.

- Adventure and excitement: Not all migrants are escaping from something. Some people actively seek out the excitement and adventure of moving to somewhere new. During the great colonial expansion, when European countries set up outposts around the world, many young people made new lives for themselves far from home in North America, India, Africa, and South East Asia.

- Spreading their message: During the 19th and 20th centuries, many Christian missionaries left their homes to move to places they felt needed to receive a Christian message. The main places they travelled to were China, Africa, and South America. Today, there are still people who migrate to other countries to spread religious messages, but more go to the developing world as aid workers to help improve education and some health services.

Forced migration: slavery and indenture

As well as those who have chosen to leave home voluntarily, such as Julia Gillard's family, many have left against their will as forced migrants. **Slavery** was definitely the worst form of forced migration. **Indenture** (see the box on page 48) had some of the aspects of slavery, but usually the indentured person became free of his or her master after a set period of time, usually seven years.

The West Africans sold into slavery in the American plantations had no control over their lives once they were captured. They and their children became the possessions of their owners with no hope for the future.

Slavery and transportation

Transportation was a means of forced migration for those convicted of criminal offences. The British government sent convicted prisoners to their colonies in North America, and then Australia, for punishment and to be a source of nearly free labour.

Between 1787 and 1868, over 160,000 convicts were transported to the British prison colonies in Australia to serve their sentences, often for what seems today to be small crimes. This may seem very harsh, but for many convicts transportation was the alternative to a sentence of death by hanging. However, as Australia today shows, many of these convicts, and their descendants, prospered – they took this as their chance to start again.

Australia today

Today, many Australians are very proud to have convict ancestry. Websites like Convict to Australia (**www.convictcentral.com**) and the CoraWeb Convict Records (**www.coraweb.com.au/convict.htm**) give details about convict ships, lists of the convicts themselves, and information about what happened to the convicts once they got to Australia. There are also lots of research tips and links to more convict sites on the internet.

Zoom in: What was the triangular trade?

Slavery grew and expanded during the 18th century because it made lots of money for those who were involved. The transactions that took place between Europe, Africa, and the American colonies became known as the triangular trade. In the first part of the triangle, ships from a European port, such as Bristol in Great Britain, were loaded with trade goods such as cloth, weapons, and rum. They would sail to West Africa where the goods were traded for human beings, who were sold to the ship captains as slaves. The second part of the triangle took the ships to the American and Caribbean plantations where the slaves were sold to work as agricultural labour. The third part of the triangular trade took the ships, now loaded with valuable goods, such as cotton, tobacco, and sugar, back to British ports. Around 10 million African slaves left their homelands as part of this horrific trading system.

Modern slavery and trafficking

The Atlantic slave trade ended during the first part of the 19th century. The Thirteenth Amendment to the US Constitution finally ended slavery in the US in 1865, following the Emancipation in 1863. Slave trade from East Africa into the Middle East ended by the 1950s. Unfortunately, slavery still exists in many parts of the world. **Debt-bondage** makes people work for others for no pay. In some places, people are still captured and sold like animals, without any control over their own lives.

Children and women suffer the most in what is now called **human trafficking**. They are sold by family members, tricked into leaving home, or even kidnapped and taken from their countries. They are then used as beggars, servants, cheap labour, or in illegal activities. The United Nations believes that over 4 million new people are trafficked against their will every year.

Luck and hard work

Through luck and hard work, some migrants who choose to leave home make great successes of their lives in new countries. Like Prime Minister Julia Gillard, many people have contributed to the social and political prosperity of their adopted homelands. These new places have changed and moulded the history of their lives.

Where should I look?

Many migrants sent letters or kept journals of their adventures because they never expected to see their families again. Some of these primary sources have been published or can be seen online. Here are a few examples of where you can look:

WEBSITES

www.historymatters.gmu.edu/d/5787

www.learnnc.org/lp/editions/nchist-colonial/1902

BOOKS

Letters from Madras: During the Years 1836–1839
by Julia Charlotte Maitland. This was first published in 1846.

Family Letters 1841–1856
by David Livingstone. This two volume book has many different editions.

Zoom in: From home town to refugee camp

Some people, for their own safety, have to leave their homes to live in appalling circumstances in refugee camps. They are usually escaping from violent political unrest that has destroyed their homes and put the lives of their families at risk. Most refugees, like these Afghans shown at a refugee camp in Pakistan (in the picture below), never know when, if ever, they will be able to return home. The United Nations High Commission for Refugees (UNHCR) estimates that there are currently more than 42 million displaced people throughout the world. For more about refugees and their problems, go to **www.unhcr.org**

Refugee camps, like this one in Pakistan, are prone to the quick spread of disease due to the cramped conditions of the people living there.

She is a woman who has successfully made the transformation from being part of a girl group to a career as a solo singer. He is a rapper, hip-hop singer, and record producer. When they announced their engagement, the media went wild. The public images of Beyoncé Knowles (born 1981) and her husband Jay-Z, sometimes written Jay Z (born 1969), are covered with the gloss of stardom and success. Is it ever possible to see the people behind the glitzy images? How can we find evidence about the real Beyoncé and Jay-Z?

Beyoncé before she was famous

It is often possible to find reliable information about people from before they were public figures. When people are still at school or university, or just starting out in their careers, they are not normally keeping a tight control of their image. Many of the "before they were famous" photographs of celebrities come from school yearbooks and childhood friends. But for Beyoncé Knowles, was there ever a time before she was even at least a little famous?

Zoom in: Who were they?

Many actors, writers, and musicians change their names. Jay-Z started his life as Shawn Carter, and has now added Beyoncé's surname to his birth name: Shawn Knowles-Carter. Beyoncé is usually only known by her first name, but officially is now Beyoncé Knowles-Carter. New names like these are known by a variety of terms: stage name, pen name, pseudonym, or alias. Here are a few old and new names:

Birth name	New name
Samuel Clemens (author)	Mark Twain
Stefani Germanotta (singer)	Lady Gaga
Theodor Geisel (writer)	Dr Seuss
Alicia Cook (singer)	Alicia Keys
Marion Morrison (actor)	John Wayne

Beyoncé Knowles and her husband Jay-Z are referred to as a celebrity couple or even as "music royalty". They married in 2008, and their daughter, Blue Ivy, was born in 2012.

The road to Destiny's Child

Beyoncé was a member of the girl group Girls Tyme (sometimes written as Girl's Tyme) at the age of just nine! When you add this to the fact that for most of her career her father Mathew has been her manager, you are left with a celebrity who grew up in the public eye, with careful control of her image. First, her fame was local in Houston, Texas, and then it spread across the United States. Eventually, she became known throughout the world as the lead singer of Destiny's Child.

Is there truth in the lyrics?

What about Jay-Z? He spent much longer trying to make it big in the music business than his wife, and was often seen at rap and MC events. But one source of evidence that a rapper and singer like Jay-Z provides for researchers is the lyrics to his early material.

Evidence that can be checked

Many of Jay-Z's lyrics claim to narrate events of his early "hard-knock" upbringing in a housing project in Brooklyn, New York. Some of these lyrics mention poverty, shootings, and drugs. But this is Jay-Z's own version of his life; some of it was probably written to create the type of image needed by a young rapper. So, this, too, might or might not represent the real Jay-Z.

Jay-Z published his autobiography, *Decoded*, in 2011. In this book, Jay-Z gave more details about his early life and how he learned from his mistakes. This evidence can be evaluated to see if it agrees with other sources. So, what other evidence is left? We know that Beyoncé and Jay-Z have been married since 2008 and have a daughter, Blue Ivy. The names of their parents and siblings are known. Their careers are well documented. Jay-Z's various business concerns are also in public records, such as his part-ownership of the Brooklyn Nets basketball team (which he talked about selling in 2013).

Giving something back

Celebrities often get involved with charitable organizations. The evidence of their involvement is usually reliable. It helps the charity and the celebrity. The celebrities get good publicity for their actions and the charities get famous, with popular people spreading their messages. Beyoncé and Jay-Z have worked for, and donated money to, various causes, such as Hurricane Katrina victims, UN water shortage programmes, and World Children's Day.

American actor Matt Damon is a celebrity who uses his image and his time to promote good causes and help others. Here he is shown, with singer Wyclef Jean, helping with food donation in the town of Cabaret in Haiti.

This shows Franklin Roosevelt accepting the nomination for president in 1932. He is holding tightly onto the lectern, and a large chair is positioned behind him.

Research roadshow: FDR – what wheelchair?

Today, when anyone in the public eye has a problem of any kind to do with his or her health or personal life, it is very hard to keep it private. Reporters spend a lot of their time trying to get the latest story. Paparazzi are paid huge amounts for photographs, but this was not always the case. Franklin Delano Roosevelt (FDR) was the US president between 1933 and 1945. He developed the disease polio when he was in his thirties. This affected his ability to walk. He had to wear leg braces and spend lots of time in a wheelchair. If he stood, he had to lean against something or someone. During his whole political career, his disability was not written about. Photographs and films did not show his wheelchair or his attempts to walk. When he was shown standing, it was never obvious that he needed help. This was considered a private matter. It was not until after FDR's death in 1945 that more details about his various health issues became public knowledge, much to many people's surprise.

Fighting the bad press

Of course, by getting involved with good causes, charities, and international organizations, celebrities like Beyoncé and Jay-Z create a positive public image. Good press can be useful when it comes to fighting negative publicity. This is particularly the case when the media reports on excessive spending and "blingy" lifestyle choices. For example, Beyoncé and Jay-Z sometimes get negative media coverage about the extravagant, flashy equipment and clothing they buy for their young daughter. When this happens, some people might remember the couple's financial support for children's charities, which shows that they understand the needs of those less fortunate.

Making a connection: Propaganda and history

Most major celebrities have whole teams of marketing and media people controlling what the public sees and finds out about them. In the future, these magazine articles, photos, and official online sources will be the documentation left behind. Knowing this, think about all the historical evidence you examine.

Considering the documentation involves asking lots of questions, particularly about whether or not it is **propaganda**. Is propaganda meant to support a particular point of view, or can the information be trusted? Does the evidence you are examining present an **objective** case? If it is objective, it will be based on well-researched facts. It will not just be influenced by personal feelings or experience. Evidence like that is **subjective**. Can evidence of that type be trusted at all? All historical researchers have to ask the following questions about the evidence they use:

• Who produced it?

• What kind of evidence is it?

• When and where was it produced?

• Why was it produced?

Depending on the answers to these questions, you can then decide how trustworthy a piece of evidence is.

Paparazzi are photographers who target celebrities in an attempt to make massive sums of money selling the photos. The ones they are paid the most for are those that show the celebrities looking bad or in embarrassing situations. Young stars like Justin Bieber need to be very careful about the situations they are photographed in.

How propaganda is used

Propaganda can be used in two ways. It can be positive. This means that it can give an unrealistically good slant to something. For example, a photograph of a celebrity that has been touched up to make the person look slimmer or more beautiful is a kind of positive propaganda. Negative propaganda is used by one side to give a bad image of their competitors or enemies. For example, in elections one political party will sometimes use certain words or phrases, or reproduce unflattering photographs, to affect how people feel about the other party. If it is done carefully enough, the voters might not even notice that their attitudes are being manipulated!

WORKING INTO HISTORY

When a 13-year-old Scottish boy arrived with his parents in the United States, he only hoped that they would be able to find enough work to buy food and pay for a place to live in. Over the next 40 years, he worked his way from bobbin winder in a cotton mill to millionaire steel producer and **philanthropist**. Andrew Carnegie's story is truly one of rags to riches. Researching his working life and that of others helps flesh out what life was like at the time.

Right time, right place

Andrew Carnegie (1835–1919) managed to get work when he arrived in the United States in 1848. He was employed in the popular occupations of the time – the railways, and then the growing iron and steel industry. The westward expansion of the United States created a need for people to work in many areas to service growing communities and provide jobs for others. By doing this, workers in these expanding areas were building and modernizing the country. They were creating the transport and communications system that made this possible.

Making a connection: American Indians – the victims of change and success

Historians often use phrases like "westward expansion" and "building a new country". These expressions ignore the fact that the frontier areas of the United States were not empty. These lands had **indigenous** populations that were constantly being displaced and disadvantaged by the arrival of new settlers. The history of the American Indian peoples was changed forever.

You can research the unfair way traditional lands were taken from the original inhabitants as the new country's population grew. Look for historical primary sources where American Indians give their opinions on what was happening to their lives. You can also look at some of the propaganda produced by the colonizing forces at the time, to get another point of view.

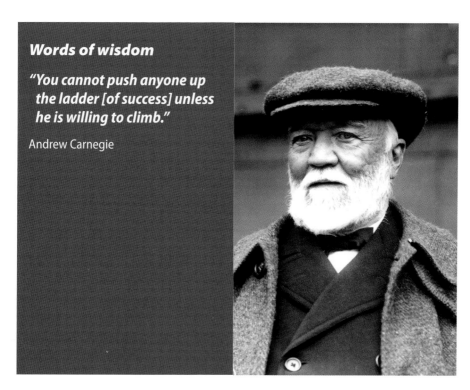

Words of wisdom

"You cannot push anyone up the ladder [of success] unless he is willing to climb."

Andrew Carnegie

The evidence of Andrew Carnegie's generosity still exists in many towns and cities that still have in use one of the 2,500 "Carnegie" free public libraries he funded.

The American Civil War (1861–1865) greatly disrupted the business and trade of the United States. Carnegie himself did not fight, but paid a substitute to serve for him. In this way, the working life of the country could continue during the conflict. By the 1870s, his investments in the coal, iron, and steel industries had made him a very rich man.

From hard work to success

Carnegie believed in hard work, and in success coming to those who were willing to make an effort. Other working people throughout history have not been as motivated or as lucky as Andrew Carnegie, but the evidence they have left behind helps us picture the times they lived in. The diaries, journals, or letters sent home by one domestic servant, farmer, factory worker, or soldier can be used to build an image of what life was like for others in the same situations. For example, Andrew Carnegie himself wrote widely about his triumphs in the world of business.

Giving something back

Andrew Carnegie was one of the richest men of his time. But he also realized how lucky he had been. By the time he died in 1919, he had given away over two thirds of what he received when he sold his businesses. Carnegie not only did what he thought was right with his wealth, but he also urged other rich and successful people to become philanthropists.

Research roadshow: Teaching on the frontier

The account of one person who did a specific job, or had specific experiences, can be useful for historical research. Laura Ingalls Wilder (1867–1957) is famous today for her autobiographical novels based on the lives of her family, as well as her later **memoirs**. From the age of 15, she taught in a small school in a village near her home. Her accounts of teaching in the 1880s can give an insight into the experiences of all teachers and their students during this period of frontier life.

Zoom in: Finding out about apprentices

Although some jobs in the past did not require any training, many professions took care to train young workers "on the job", and these young workers became known as apprentices. Someone who was fully qualified in the job was known as a "master". He would take on a young person, the "apprentice", and give them a number of years of training, usually seven. At the end of this time, the apprentice would be able to do the job on his own. There were legal documents called **indentures** relating to what the apprenticeship would consist of, and more documents when the apprenticeship ended. Many of these can be found indexed by name and profession and can be seen online or in museums and archives. Apprenticeships still exist in some places today, although the process is very different!

Where should I look?

There are records and documents for many different jobs and professions – as the girl and her grandmother in this picture, below, are discovering. Some jobs, such as those in medicine and the law, have professional bodies that regulate entry and keep records. There are companies that keep full archives including information about employees. If the companies no longer exist, these records might now be deposited in local record offices or museums.

It can also be possible to read about some jobs in the words of people who performed them. During the 20th century, one of the most famous collections of written material about everyday life in Britain was built up. It is called Mass Observation. From 1937 until 1950, diaries were kept by many different people in all walks of life. The Mass Observation Archive is now at the University of Sussex. Find out about it at on the following site: **www.massobs.org.uk**

Oral history projects involve the real recorded voices of men, women, and children. This evidence is a useful secondary source. But remember, those being interviewed usually only answer the questions they are asked. This can have an effect on the reliability of the information. For example, someone interviewing an elderly person who attended a one-room school may not ask about how they got to school. This does not mean that the journey was easy or uneventful.

ARE WE ALL RELATED?

In AD 814, the crowned king of the Franks died. During the previous 40 years, he had founded the Holy Roman Empire, which would continue to exist in one form or another until 1806. He had also unified and Christianized much of Europe. This king was Charlemagne (AD 742–814), and there are those who think we are all, in some way, related to him.

Charlemagne's descendants

Louis, Charlemagne's son, partitioned off his land to his sons, and they did the same for the next generation, and so on. So, the history of Charlemagne's descendants, the Carolingians, became the history of the various duchies, counties, and provinces of Europe. But how does this make us all related to Charlemagne? In fact, it's not in the geography at all; it's in the maths.

The further back, the more ancestors! *i*

The number of ancestors every person has gets bigger every generation back in time. For example, you have two parents, but you have four grandparents, eight great-grandparents, and 16 great-great-grandparents. Imagine how many this could be by the time you go back over 1,200 years to AD 800!

Ancestor in AD 800

In the late 1990s, Dr Joseph Chang, of Yale University, used various mathematical models to work out that every European alive today has more ancestors than the total amount of people who have ever lived! He also calculated that every European living between about AD 300 and AD 800 is related to every person of European descent alive today. Since the first Holy Roman Emperor was the most famous person alive in Europe in AD 800, it is easy to say that we are all related to Charlemagne. But it is just as true of his servants and his wife!

On Christmas Day 800 CE, Pope Leo III crowned Charlemagne Holy Roman Emperor at the cathedral in Aachen in present-day Germany. This picture shows a stained-glass representation of Charlemagne.

Zoom in: Passengers of the Mayflower

It does not take very many generations for a small number of people to have a huge number of descendants. The *Mayflower*, which carried the pilgrims from Plymouth in Devon to Massachusetts in the American colonies in 1620, had 102 passengers. Today, academics estimate that there are 35 million descendants of those original settlers.

Before Charlemagne

How far can people's history be traced back? The answer is, everyone's ancestry goes back to the first people who gradually spread out from Africa to populate the world. But you can't find this answer using geography or maths – you need biology.

Most people think of **DNA** as something used by the police to help catch criminals. How can it help people understand their ancestry? Individuals **inherit** all of their characteristics from their parents in the form of **genes**: 23 genes from the mother and 23 genes from the father. From the time of the first human beings, this inheritance has been passed in the genes from generation to generation. DNA stores and copies exactly this inherited genetic information in cells of the body. **Geneticists** and **anthropologists** use DNA information to trace the ancestry of humankind much further back than Charlemagne. DNA samples collected from ancient bones and living populations have made it possible to map the expansion worldwide of the earliest people from their original home in prehistoric Africa.

Zoom in: DNA from your mother and your father

Your matrilineal DNA is the DNA you inherit from your mother. It is also called mitochondrial DNA. Your patrilineal DNA is the DNA you inherit from your father. It is also known as Y-chromosome DNA. Men inherit the DNA pairing "XY" and women the DNA pairing "XX" from their parents. Because a woman inherits an "X" from each of her parents, this means she never inherits patrilineal DNA from her father.

What can DNA tell us?

DNA can be used to link individuals together as family members over many generations. Certain parts of a person's DNA, known as markers, only exist in specific populations. They can be used to identify which areas of the world someone's ancestry comes from. For example, a DNA test might be able to tell a person that his or her ancestry over hundreds of generations is 75 per cent Western European and 25 per cent sub-Saharan African.

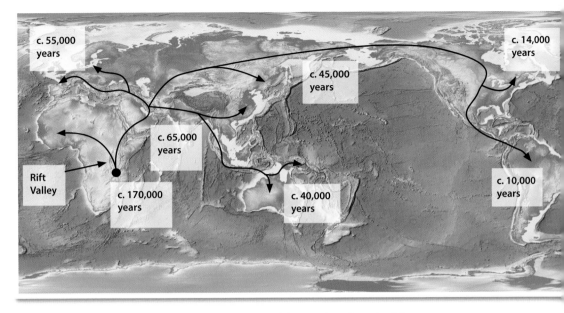

c. 55,000 years

c. 14,000 years

c. 45,000 years

c. 65,000 years

Rift Valley

c. 170,000 years

c. 40,000 years

c. 10,000 years

This map shows how the earliest humans probably spread out from the Rift Valley in Africa (on the far left of the picture) from about 200,000 years ago. Over time, they eventually populated the world. DNA information and archaeological discoveries have been used to help create this map.

Prehistory and history

i

The term "prehistory" is used to describe the period on Earth before there were written records. To find out about prehistory, and the people who lived in prehistoric times, it is necessary to study things we can find that they left behind. Tools, bones, cave paintings, and the remains of stone and wooden structures, help build up a picture of prehistoric peoples' lives. These objects are all primary sources.

We have already seen that history depends on written accounts of events. Eventually, various civilizations developed forms of writing and they have left written records of their lives. The first written histories we have of real events are the descriptions of the wars between Greece and Persia. These were written in the 5th century BC by a Greek man, Herodotus.

DNA confirms a king

In September 2012, British **archaeologists** made an amazing discovery. They thought that bones they had excavated in the city of Leicester were those of King Richard III, who had died nearby, at the Battle of Bosworth in 1485. The place they found the skeleton, the dating of the bones, the twisting of the skeleton's spine, and the evidence of battle wounds all pointed to it being Richard.

But how could archaeologists confirm their suspicions? They called in historians, genealogists, and DNA experts. The genealogists knew that Richard had no direct descendants as his only children had died without having children themselves. Luckily, they were able to trace some descendants of Richard's siblings. Canadian furniture maker Michael Ibsen (shown in the picture opposite) was one of the people whose DNA was compared with the DNA of the skeleton. He is a confirmed direct descendant, 17 generations down, from Richard's sister, Anne of York, Duchess of Exeter.

Research roadshow: Thomas Jefferson's surprising DNA

For many years, the descendants of Sally Hemmings, a slave owned by US President Thomas Jefferson, had claimed that Jefferson was the father of Sally's children. They believed that Jefferson had a relationship with her after his wife died. They even held family reunions of all the Hemmings-Jefferson descendants. Nearly 200 years after those original children were born, DNA testing gave the descendants the answer they had hoped for. They did have Jefferson ancestry.

Many family history researchers without famous ancestors also use DNA testing to link family groups of the same name. This is done through the testing of male family members with the same surname using Y-chromosome DNA matching. The Guild of One-Name Studies (GOONS) has information on its website about many of these name-specific DNA projects. See the site **www.one-name.org**

DNA evidence confirmed that the skeleton discovered under a car park in the city of Leicester was that of King Richard III. In February 2013, the results were in – and they were a match! A 21st-century technique had helped to identify a missing king, over 500 years after his death. This model was made by a facial reconstruction technique using the skull from the car park skeleton.

Zoom in: Facial reconstruction techniques

The method known as forensic facial reconstruction can be used to create a three-dimensional model of a person's face and head using a skull. It can be used to establish identity in criminal and missing persons' cases when a skeleton is discovered and DNA testing is not a good option. It is also used in some cases to help us look at what the features of our prehistoric and historic ancestors might have looked like. In the early days of this technique, it was very time-consuming and hundreds of measurement had to be taken. Today, the experts usually use medical CT scans and computer software to give them average tissue depth measurements. An artist then adds clay to a model of the actual skull. Unfortunately, reconstructions cannot tell you about the person's weight, or if they had wrinkles or scars. Look online to see how the technique gradually builds up a human face.

YOU HAVE A HISTORY

Your personal history

Your own personal history starts the day you are born and lasts until the day you die. It will partly be the product of the histories of your parents and their parents back through the generations. Your history will overlap with and influence other people's histories. All through this time, your existence will create the evidence and documentation of your life.

Your evidence trail

The evidence that documents your life starts before you are born with the medical records of your mother's pregnancy. You will then generate a birth certificate, and more medical history, including vaccination records. Religious ceremonies, like a baptism or a bar mitzvah, may also create written documentation.

When you start your education, the build-up of evidence really accelerates. All the schools you attend will have records relating to your time with them. Tests and examinations will also create important documents. You may add to this growing personal archive with a university degree certificate or other diplomas.

Zoom in: Digital records don't go away

Although you will try hard to preserve the important documentation of your life, there may be digital records you wished never existed. Once something gets into the cyber world, it is very hard to get rid of it. That silly photograph of you with a friend, or a particular YouTube or Facebook posting, might seem funny at the time, but a university admissions officer or future employer might not think so in five or six years. Make sure you think before you do something you may regret later.

More records

When you enter the world of work, your employers will keep records of your time with them. These will be used for their own records and certain records will be used for the purpose of taxation or other financial obligations. Marriage or home ownership could create yet more documentation.

You may need to produce items such as educational certificates when you apply for jobs or want to do further study. Your birth certificate will be needed when you apply for a passport or if you decide to get married. To be safe, it is best to keep all of this important documentation in several formats. The original paper copies can be stored in a filing cabinet or a metal box. Digital scans can be kept on your computer and also stored in the cloud, or on a CD, or on an external hard drive.

Remember, many people who were born at the beginning of the 21st century have every possibility of living into their nineties, if not longer. Your history, and the documents that support it, will need to be safeguarded for a very long time. As well as keeping a record of your life for others, you may need – or, at least may be very interested – in looking through the documents in the future!

Life events, such as weddings, can generate a lot of evidence, including certificates, photographs, and special clothing. Make sure you keep track of who appears in school or family photos. You know all the names now, but you might not remember in 30 years' time.

BECOME YOUR FAMILY'S HISTORIAN

Where can I look?

You can become your family's historian by researching the people in the family's past and the events that shaped their lives. Here are some ideas about where you can look to start documenting your family:

- Census returns: These are available for the UK at 10-year intervals, from 1841. The only year not available is 1941, where there was no census carried out, partly as a result of World War II. They are only released to the public after 100 years, so 1841 to 1911 can now be examined online, in county record offices, and in some libraries.

- National birth, marriage, and death records: From 1837, it became a legal requirement in the UK to register all births, marriages, and deaths. These records are also available online, in record offices and in some libraries. Before 1837, marriages and burials were recorded in church or synagogue registers. Many of these parish registers have been copied out to help you find information easier, and some are indexed.

- Groups and societies: There are family history and local history societies in most countries that create resources for their members to use. In the UK, many local groups are members of the Federation of Family History Societies. See **www.ffhs.org.uk** to find a family or local history society near you or in the area where your family comes from.

Do remember, there are free sites on the internet that you can research for family history information, but others require payment or even expensive membership fees. Many public libraries and local record offices have subscriptions to these sites, which they allow their members to use free of charge.

This kind of family history record sheet (opposite) is called a **pedigree** chart. It shows the direct ancestors from one particular person. You put the name of the person whose pedigree the form will represent in the middle box on the left. You then work right, back through the earlier generations, filling in the person's parents, then grandparents, then great-grandparents, and so on. Names are the most important, but also fill in any birth, marriage, and death dates you can find, and the places where these events took place.

Example of a pedigree chart

			16	Father of 8
				B:
				D:
	8	Father of 4	17	Mother of 8
		B:		B:
		P:		D:
		M:	18	Father of 9
		D:		B:
		P:		D:
4	Father of 2	9	Mother of 4	19	Mother of 9
	B:		B:		B:
	P:		P:		D:
	M:		D:	20	Father of 10
	D:		P:		B:
	P:	10	Father of 5		D:
			B:	21	Mother of 10
			P:		B:
			M:		D:
	5	Mother of 2		D:	22	Father of 11
		B:	11	Mother of 5		B:
		P:		B:		D:
		M:		P:	23	Mother of 11
		D:		D:		B:
		P:		P:		D:

Father of 1
B:
P:
M:
D:
P:

1 A. Person

B: Birth
P: Place
M: Marriage
D: Died
P: Place

Mother of 1
B:
P::
D:
P:

			24	Father of 12
				B:
				D:
	12	Father of 6	25	Mother of 12
		B:		B:
		P:		D:
		M:	26	Father of 13
		P:		B:
6	Father of 3	13	Mother of 6		D:
	B:		B:	27	Mother of 13
	P:		P:		B:
	M:		D:		D:
	D:		P:	28	Father of 14
	P:	14	Father of 7		B:
			B:		D:
			P:	29	Mother of 14
			M:		B:
	7	Mother of 3		D:		D:
		B:		P:	30	Father of 15
		P:	15	Mother of 7		B:
		D:		B:		D:
		P:		P:	31	Mother of 15
				D:		B:
				P:		D:

GLOSSARY

Allies group of countries that fought against Germany and its supporters

ancestor person someone is descended from. Your parents are your ancestors.

anthropologist someone who studies anthropology, the science of the physical and cultural development of humankind

apartheid separating people because of their race

archaeologist person who studies ancient peoples and their culture

archive collection of historical documents or records

autobiography story of one person's life, written by that person

biopic film that tells the story of a specific real person

Cenotaph monument in London that stands as a memorial to all British and Commonwealth war dead

census official counting of the population, and collection of related statistics

civil registration legally compulsory registration of life events

civil servant central government employee

colonial related to a colony (territory in one country, controlled by another country)

compulsory required or necessary

context conditions or events that can affect something's meaning

debt-bondage forced work for little or no money to pay back money already owed

descendant person descended from an ancestor. You are your parents' descendant.

dispatches official messages sent by an officer from a war zone

displaced persons those who have had to move away from their homes

DNA (deoxyribonucleic acid) molecule that forms chromosomes and combines to make genes

document in history, a written piece of evidence

ethnicity of a background or culture

evaluate work out if something is important or true

evidence in history, anything that helps create an accurate picture of the past

family tree chart or diagram showing the ancestry and relationships of a family

gene basic unit in the body that leads to the inheritance of characteristics

genealogist someone who is an expert at genealogy, the study of family ancestries and histories

geneticist biological scientist who studies genes and how they work

human trafficking moving, trading, and even selling people

indenture (slavery) bound by contract to work for a certain amount of time

indentures (apprenticeship) documents or contracts dented at the edges binding someone to an apprenticeship

indigenous native to a certain place

inherit pass from one generation to the next

logbook written record officially kept by those in the military or in education to record daily happenings

memoir someone's personal record of events he or she has experienced

memorial something designed as a way of remembering the dead

migrant person who migrates (moves) from one place to another

militia military force made up of civilian volunteers from a local area

missionary somebody sent somewhere to perform religious or charity work

obituary written notice of a person's death, usually with biographical details

objective judging something as fairly as possible based on trustworthy evidence

oral history historical evidence recorded on tape or written down as spoken

pedigree genealogical record of an ancestral line

persecution being cruelly treated, usually for religious, political, or racial reasons

philanthropist person who tries to help others through charitable acts, such as donations of money to a "good" cause

primary source historical source that dates from the period itself

propaganda material that is deliberately slanted in a positive or a negative way

Quaker member of a Christian group called the Society of Friends

recluse someone who hides away from others

reliable likely to be true or accurate

secondary source historical source produced after the event

slavery state of those who are the property of and completely under the control of their owner

social history history of the everyday family life of people

subjective judging something based on evidence that might not be accurate or trustworthy, in particular personal opinions or feelings

FIND OUT MORE

Books

Slavery and the Slave Trade (Research It!), Richard Spilsbury (Heinemann Library, 2010)

Twentieth Century (Collins History), Alf Wilkinson *et al* (Collins, 2010)

World War I (Research It!), Stewart Ross (Heinemann Library, 2010)

World War II (Research It!), Andrew Langley (Heinemann Library, 2010)

Magazines

BBC History Magazine
This highly illustrated magazine is full of interesting articles about people and events. It is also available for tablets and in an e-book format.

Family Tree Magazine
This magazine has plenty of good information on how to research your own family or find out about others from the past. It has useful articles, and reviews of books and online resources.

Hindsight Magazine
This magazine is aimed mainly at GCSE history students, but it has many interesting articles written by historians about the 20th century and its important historical figures. The articles include primary sources, such as eyewitness accounts, and other documentary evidence.

Who Do You Think You Are?
This magazine supports the television programme where celebrities trace parts of their family trees. As well as including information that does not appear on the programmes, the magazine has articles on other family history subjects, such as DNA and dating photographs.

Websites

www.bbc.co.uk/bitesize/ks3/history
This website covers many important periods in history, including the Tudors and Stuarts, the Industrial Revolution, and the 20th century.

www.bbc.co.uk/history/historic_figures
Full of short biographies of hundreds of historic figures, such as Winston S. Churchill, Florence Nightingale, Charlemagne, and Martin Luther King, Jr.

www.movingpeoplechangingplaces.org
This website gives a wealth of information about all aspects of migration. There are personal stories and many suggested sources for further research.

www.nationalarchives.gov.uk/education/topics/topics-ks3.htm
The National Archives website can be used to find many topics you may be interested in or happen to be studying. The site features scans of original documents and other primary sources that you can use to support your research.

Further research

Learn more about people and the history of their lives by doing further research on these topics, events, and individuals:

- Research the history of the Olympic Games, the Paralympic Movement, and other major sporting competitions. Find out about the people involved in developing and participating in these events.

- Look into the people and places involved in the development of some of the major food and product crops in the world, such as cotton, sugar, rubber, and wheat.

- Write down some of the names of roads, buildings, and even towns in your area that seem to be named after people. See if you can find out about them and their histories.

- See if there are any war memorials near where you live. If there are, find out if the details on them have been recorded. If not, consider making this a local history project.

- Most countries have had people move in from other places, as well as others leaving to find new homes. Research your country or area to find out about the different groups of people who have arrived and left over the years.

INDEX